SHERLOCK HOLMES'
Elementary Puzzles

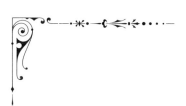

THIS IS A CARLTON BOOK

Published by Carlton Books Ltd
20 Mortimer Street
London W1T 3JW

Copyright © 2014 Carlton Books Ltd

A CIP catalogue for this book is available from the British Library.

ISBN 978-1-78097-578-8

Project editor: Richard Wolfrik Galland
Text and puzzles: Tim Dedopulos
Design: James Pople
Production: Dawn Cameron

Full-page original artworks: Rebecca Wright
Additional art and watercolouring: Chris Gould

The publishers would like to thank Mary Evans Picture Library for their
kind permission to reproduce the pictures in this book which appear on
the following pages:

12, 16, 18, 25, 32, 43, 45, 46, 51, 56, 57, 59, 61, 62, 63, 64, 65, 66, 67, 68, 72, 76, 77,
78, 81, 86, 87, 88, 91, 92, 93, 94, 114, 121, 122, 124, 131, 135, 137 & 143

Every effort has been made to acknowledge correctly and contact the source
and/or copyright holder of each picture and Carlton Books Limited apologises
for any unintentional errors or omissions, which will be corrected in future
editions of this book.

Content previously published as *The Sherlock Holmes Puzzle Collection*.

Printed in Dubai

SHERLOCK HOLMES'

Elementary Puzzles

Riddles, enigmas and challenges inspired
by the world's greatest crime-solver

Dr John Watson

CARLTON
BOOKS

CONTENTS

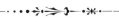

STRAIGHTFORWARD

Question   Answer

INTRODUCTION

The name of my dear friend and companion Mr. Sherlock Holmes is familiar to all who possess any interest whatsoever in the field of criminal investigation. Indeed, there are some weeks where it hardly seems possible to pick up a newspaper without seeing his name splashed luridly across the front page. Unlike so many, however, his renown is justly deserved – not for nothing has he frequently been heralded as England's greatest detective, living or dead. Personally, I suspect that his abilities are unmatched anywhere in the world at this time.

I myself have been fortunate enough to share in Holmes' extraordinary adventures, and if I have been unable to rival his insight, I have consoled myself by acting as his de facto chronicler. I also flatter myself a little with the notion that I have, betimes, provided some little warmth of human companionship. We have spent many years, on and off, sharing rooms at 221b Baker Street, and I like to think that the experience has enriched both our existences. My name, though it is of little matter, is John Watson, and I am by profession a doctor.

My dear friend has long had a passionate ambition to improve the minds of humanity. He has often talked about writing a book that will help to instil the habits which he considers so absolutely vital to the art of deduction. Such a tome would be a revolutionary step in the history of mankind, and would most certainly address observation, logical analysis, criminal behaviour, scientific and mathematical knowledge, clear thinking, and much more besides. Alas, it has yet to materialise, for the world is full of villainy, and Sherlock Holmes is ever drawn to the solution of very real problems.

But over the course of our adventures, Holmes has never given up on the cause of improving my modest faculties. On innumerable occasions, he has presented me with opportunities to engage my mind, and solve some problem or other which to him is perfectly clear from the information already available. These trials have sometimes been quite taxing, and have not always come at a welcome moment, but I have engaged in all of them to the very best of my abilities. To do otherwise would be to dishonour the very generous gift my friend is making me in devoting time to my analytical improvement.

In truth, I do believe that his ministrations have indeed helped. I consider myself to be more aware than I was in my youth, and less prone to hasty assessments and faulty conclusions. If I have gained any greater talent in these areas, it is entirely thanks to the efforts that my friend has exerted on my behalf, for it is most certainly not an area for which I am naturally disposed. Give me a sickly patient, and I feel absolutely confident of swiftly arriving at the appropriate diagnosis and, to the limits provided by medical science, of attaining a successful recovery for the poor unfortunate. But my mind does not turn naturally to criminality, violence or deception. If this were a perfect world, then we would all co-exist in genial and honourable honesty, and I would be perfectly suited for the same. Alas, that is far from the case, and my dear friend is far better adapted to the murky undertows of the real world than I.

Still, as I have already attested, Holmes' little trials have had a beneficial effect even on me. For one who is more readily disposed to such efforts, the results may well be commensurately powerful. Thus, I have taken the liberty of assembling this collection.

Working assiduously from my notes, I have compiled somewhere in the region of one hundred and fifty of the puzzles that Holmes has set me over the years. I have been assiduous in ensuring that I have described the situation as I first encountered it, with all pertinent information reproduced. The answers are as detailed as I can usefully make them. Some I managed to answer successfully myself; for others, I have reproduced Holmes' explanations as accurately as my notes permit.

To improve the accessibility a little, I have attempted to order the trials into approximate groupings of difficulty – elementary, straightforward, cunning and fiendish, to be exact. Holmes has a devious mind, and there were times when he was entirely determined to baffle me, whilst

on other occasions, the problems were simple enough
to serve as illustrative examples of certain principles. I
believe that I have broadly succeeded in classifying the
difficulty of his riddles, but I beg your indulgence in so
uncertain a matter. Every question is easy, if you know the
answer, and the opposite holds equally true.

If is my fervent hope that you will find this little volume
enlightening and amusingly diverting. If it may prove
to sharpen your deductive sense a little, that would be
all the vindication that I could ever possibly wish; all
the credit for such improvement would be due Holmes
himself. I, as always, am content to be just the scribe.
I have taken every effort to ensure that the problems
are all amenable to fair solution, but if by some remote
happenchance that should prove not the case, it must be
clear that the blame lies entirely on my shoulders, and
that none should devolve to my dear companion.

My friends, it is with very real pleasure that I present to
you this volume of the puzzles of Mr. Sherlock Holmes.

I remain, as always, your servant,

Dr John H. Watson.

ELEMENTARY

PUZZLES

"In solving problems of this sort, the grand thing is to be able to reason backwards."

Sherlock Holmes

A MATTER OF IDENTITY

As we were walking through Regent's Park one afternoon, on our way to St. John's Wood, Holmes drew my attention to a pair of young women engaged in earnest conversation with a somewhat older man.

"Observe those ladies, Watson. What can you tell me about them?"

I studied them closely. They were as alike as peas in a pod, identical in facial structure, deportment, dress and coiffure. I said as much to my companion, and asserted that they surely had to be twins.

"Indeed?" Holmes looked amused. "For a fact, I can tell you that Louise and Lisa Barnes share the same mother, the same father, and the same precise day of birth, but I'm afraid you are utterly wrong. They are most certainly not twins."

Can you explain?

SOLUTION ON PAGE 96

A DIFFICULT AGE

"Logic is paramount, Watson."
Sherlock Holmes was in a thoughtful mood, pacing slowly up and down the length of the sitting room, pipe firmly in hand. "The better able you are to pick apart a problem in your mind and evaluate all of the ramifications it encompasses, the stronger will be your deductive reasoning."

"Of course," I said.

"So, then. Let us say that I know of a particular fellow. Today is a singular occasion, for two days ago, he was 25 years of age, but next year, he will be 28.

How is such a thing possible?"

SOLUTION ON PAGE  97

COLD FEET

"You've noticed, I dare say, at night, when the flat is cold, that the carpeted floor here in the sitting room feels much warmer than the tiled floor in the bathroom," said Holmes.

"Quite so," I agreed.

"Have you given any thought to why that ought to be the case?"

"Well, the carpet..." I began, trailing off as I realised I had not actually considered the matter.

"But surely you cannot think that the carpet is any different temperature to the tile. The flat is uniformly heated, after all."

"Of course not."

"So why the difference, then?"

SOLUTION ON PAGE 97

THE FIRST CURIOSITY

olmes has on occasion extolled the virtues of absurdity as a way of breaking free of the confines of regimented thinking. "Watson," he told me once, "the ridiculous is one of the best methods to shatter the iron confines of pedestrian thought."

With that in mind, he engaged in a programme of springing baffling and sometimes ludicrous problems on me at moments when I least expected them.

The first caught me completely unawares.

"I have considered commissioning a house with windows facing south on all four sides," Holmes declared, to my amazement. "Do you think this is a good idea?"

SOLUTION ON PAGE 98

THE FOOL

Inspector Lestrade had inveigled Holmes and myself into going with him to Dawes Heath in Essex, where a consignment of goose lard had gone missing under rather peculiar circumstances. We were making our way through the small village when Lestrade suddenly hooted with laughter.

"You have to see this, Holmes." He beckoned us over to a small, disreputable shack, outside of which a poor wretch was whittling a piece of bark. "This chap is the village idiot," Lestrade said quietly. "He's got not the first clue. Offered the choice between a penny and a shilling, he'll pick the penny every time."

"Is that so?" Holmes sounded amused.

"Watch," said the Inspector. He fished in his pocket for a moment, and then produced the two coins, and offered them grandly to the whittling local. The chap leapt up, and with great noises of appreciation, took the penny and went cavorting off with it, crowing over its coppery sheen. Lestrade looked most pleased with himself.

"If there's a fool here," Holmes said archly, "it's not that fellow."

What did he mean?

SOLUTION ON PAGE 99

RABBIT RACE

"Did you ever engage in a rabbit race?" Holmes' rather peculiar question brought me up short, and I stopped in the street to stare at him. "Why do you ask?"

"I was considering an illustrative question for you, my dear Watson," he said, "such matters can be somewhat revealing."

I shrugged. "Pray continue, if my lack of the requisite experience does not invalidate the problem."

"Not in the least, the problem is quite elementary. Imagine then, if you will, a pair of quite companionable rabbits of long-standing familiarity to each other. Instructed to race for the amusement of children, they are happy enough to amble along at the same speed, keeping each other company and, inevitably, yielding a dead heat."

"That seems plausible enough," I ventured.

"After the race, one of the judges notes that the first half and second half were run in the same time, and that the last quarter lasted as long as the penultimate. If the first three quarters took 6¾ minutes, how long was the entire race?"

SOLUTION ON PAGE 99

THE BARREL

"Come Watson," said Holmes. "Let's test your mental musculature with a simple challenge."

"Very well," I replied.

"Imagine you are faced with a sizeable, open-topped barrel of water," Holmes instructed me. "You know that it is close to being half-full, but you do not know whether it is exactly so, or more or less. With no instrument available with which to measure the depth of the water, can you devise a means to ascertain its state?"

SOLUTION ON PAGE 100

THE FIRST MENTAL TRIAL

"**M**y dear Watson, a keen mind must be able to follow a thread of logic through convoluted labyrinths at which even an Ariadne would quail."

"I dare say that's true," said I. "Do I assume that means you have some trial for me?"

"I couldn't say," replied Holmes, "but if you did, that assumption would be well founded."

"Very well," I said. "Pray, go ahead."

"This should prove a gentle warm-up. There is something you own that it is yours, and always has been. Despite this, all your friends use it, whilst you yourself rarely get to make use of it at all. What am I talking about?"

SOLUTION ON PAGE **100**

WHISTLER

"**Y**ou must have noticed that a kettle gets quieter shortly before it boils," Holmes said.

I nodded agreeably.

"Why is that, would you think?"

SOLUTION ON PAGE **101**

THE FIRST LITERAL ODDITY

"**A**s you must be aware, with this volume in your hands, I have some very meagre scrapings of ability in the weaving of sentences. I hesitate to call my facility, such as it is, a talent, but I hope I have managed to document my friend's extraordinary adventures in an amusing manner.

In amongst his efforts at improving my very basic skills of deduction and investigation, Holmes from time to time would challenge my linguistic facility. Whilst this was undoubtedly a change of pace from some of his little challenges, he none the less managed to ensure that his wordplay provided me with a genuine test. These trials of his may be diverting to you, and are offered in that spirit.

I was minding my own business one morning, munching on a piece of Mrs. Hudson's toast, when Holmes suddenly barked "Honorificabilitudinitatibus!"

I managed to splutter "I beg your pardon?"

"Honorificabilitudinitatibus, Watson. 'Of honour', more familiarly. You may place some blame for its inclusion in the canon of English at the feet of Master Shakespeare. Or if that monstrosity is not to your taste, how about 'unimaginatively', 'verisimilitudes', or 'parasitological'?

"I don't follow you," I said.

"What do those words have in common, man?
It should be simplicity itself for a fellow of your abilities."

SOLUTION ON PAGE  **101**

ELEMENTARY GEOMETRY

One morning, as we were heading into South London, Holmes said to me, "A grasp of elementary geometry is a powerful weapon in the fight against crime."

I admitted that this sounded like sage advice, given the occasional need to apprehend villains by the swiftest route.

"There are other purposes as well," Holmes admonished.

"Of course," I said.

"So here is a basic little matter for you. Assume you are a villain, robbing a warehouse near a straight stretch of the river. Your plan is to carry your goods to the riverside, where a confederate is waiting with a small boat, and then have him sail off casually while you make your way back to a cab, waiting at the entrance to the dock. Obviously you need to make sure that your total route is the shortest possible, as every second may count. How would you go about calculating the precise location of the boat along the river-bank?"

SOLUTION ON PAGE  102

THE MEAL

There was one occasion where I did manage to stump the great Sherlock Holmes with a puzzle that vexed him most mightily. The problem is simple. A woman presented a man with some food. He duly ate it. As a direct and absolute consequence of eating it, he died. If he had not eaten it, his death would have been averted.

As I explained in response to Holmes' terse questioning, the food was perfectly pleasant. It was not in the least bit toxic or deleterious, nor did it convey any disease or ailment. It was not stolen, or subject to mistaken identity, and no-one later came looking for it. The man consumed the food successfully, without any discomfort, and with no obstruction of the air passages. In fact, he enjoyed it, and his death was greatly delayed. Never the less, the food he consumed on that specific occasion was solely responsible for his demise.

Can you see the answer that even the world's greatest detective could not?

SOLUTION ON PAGE 103

EUREKA

"**J**oin me in a little thought exercise about fluid dynamics, Watson."

Holmes appeared to be in good humour, and I readily agreed to his suggestion.

"If you place a small boat-like vessel into a tank of water, it will displace a weight of water equal to its own, causing the water level to rise. So it must be clear that if you then put a steel weight inside the vessel, the water level will rise further."

"Indeed."

"So what do you think would happen if you were to throw the weight over the side of the vessel, down into the water? Would the water level rise, remain unchanged, or fall?"

SOLUTION ON PAGE 104

REGENT STREET

As we were travelling along Regent Street one evening, Holmes paused to engage a painter who, with his mate, was just finishing up the work of renewing the lamp posts along the street.

Holmes quickly ascertained that the men had been apportioned the east and west sides of the street. One had arrived early, and made a start, but had picked the wrong side. His companion arrived after three posts had been completed, and the chap moved back to start on the correct side. We caught them as they were finishing, and to help speed the process up, the tardier man had switched to his mate's side at the end, and painted six posts for him.

Thus completed, the men were idly curious as to which had painted the more posts, the early fellow or the tardy one, and by how many. They confirmed that there were the same number of posts on both sides

Holmes declared the matter elementary, and indicated I should explain. What would your answer have been?

SOLUTION ON PAGE  104

RIDER

"Allow me to vex you with a little question about a horseback journey," Holmes said to me.

"I am not a comfortable rider these days," I said.

"That is of no matter. It will not affect your appreciation of the question."

I nodded. "Very well."

"On a journey in the country, you travel to your destination at a reasonably sprightly 12 miles per hour. On the return, you set a more modest pace, in deference to your steed's exertions, and manage just 8 miles per hour. What is your average speed for the journey?"

SOLUTION ON PAGE 105

THE SECOND MENTAL TRIAL

"I am going out for a while, Watson." "I trust you will have a congenial time," I replied.

"I feel it can be made more profitable by the combination of a little business with a little mental work on your part," Holmes told me.

"Oh?"

"I will cheerfully buy you a cup of tea if you meet me on the corner of the Strand at a precise time."

"And when is that?"

"That should be an elementary matter for you to deduce, my friend. Three hours before the meeting time is as long after three in the morning as it is in advance of three in the afternoon. Will I see you there?"

I assured him that he would. Could you have done the same?

SOLUTION ON PAGE 106

THE GANG

One evening, after Sherlock Holmes and myself had provided some assistance to Scotland Yard on a matter of some delicacy, Inspector Lestrade took the opportunity to challenge my companion with what he hoped would prove a vexatious riddle. His hopes were unfounded of course, but I'm sure that comes as no surprise.

"I was at a break-in yesterday, Mr. Holmes," began the Inspector. "Nasty business. A group of burly young men apprehended a man and his wife outside their home, and forcibly restrained them there. Meanwhile, two of their number kicked the door straight off its hinges and charged in there. They came out a few minutes later with the couple's most precious treasure. Then, to top it all off, rather than scarpering like your usual villain would, they handed their loot over to the weeping wife, and went about their business. I saw the whole thing, but I didn't make even a single arrest. What do you make of that?"

SOLUTION ON PAGE 106

THE HAMPSTEAD TWINS

We returned to 221b Baker Street late one evening, after having spent the day chasing around Blackheath. Mrs Hudson was kind enough to bring us a very welcome pot of tea, and a plate of biscuits. Before leaving, she looked across at Holmes and myself.

"Have I ever told you fine gents about my niece Katie?"

I shook my head, but Holmes recalled that she was a maid for a couple somewhere up in Hampstead.

"That's her," said Mrs. Hudson. "She was telling me last week that the youngsters of the family had just been celebrating their birthdays. Twins, they are, a boy and a girl. Born within fifteen minutes of each other. But the younger one's birthday came two clear days before the elder's. Can you make sense of it?"

SOLUTION ON PAGE

THE FIRST PORTMANTEAU

"Observation, analysis, deduction." Holmes punctuated each word with a brisk rap on the arm of his chair. "These are the cornerstones of the art of investigation. I want you to study this little arrangement I've had drawn, Watson."

I agreed to do so of course, but confessed a certain bemusement as to what I was looking for. I have copied it for you, of course.

"It is a visual portmanteau, old chap. The image contains a number of clues referring to a rather well-known spot in London. Different elements of the picture show different aspects of the location, and in combination, there is only one place on Earth where it could possibly be. You should be able to identify it rather easily, I think."

I looked again, and you know, Holmes was right. There was only one place the image could refer to. Do you know where?

SOLUTION ON PAGE  108

THE THIRD MENTAL TRIAL

"**M**y dear Watson, will you understand my meaning when I inform you that an entirely hypothetical acquaintance of mine, Alfie, told me about a bus journey he had recently made."

"I see," I said. "This is by way of a puzzle."

"Quite so. Alfie told me that his bus was quite busy, and he was initially unable to seat himself. His fortunes changed at the half-way mark however, and he finally got the chance to take the weight off his feet. When he had just one half as far to go again to his destination as the distance for which he had been seated, an infirm gentleman boarded the bus, and Alfie generously gave up his place for the man. At the end of his journey, he decided to calculate the proportion for which he had managed to avoid standing. Can you tell me what it was?"

SOLUTION ON PAGE  109

CATFORD

"I heard of a schoolmistress, down in Catford, with a rather peculiar morning ceremonial," Holmes told me.

"The mind boggles," I replied. Catford can be a queer place, although it is rightly famed for its historic curry house.

"It is her habit," he continued, "to start the school day with a series of polite bows. Each boy must bow to each other boy, and then to each girl, and then to the teacher. Likewise, each girl must bow to each other girl, and then to each boy, and then to the teacher. The whole process requires 900 obeisances. If I tell you that there are twice as many girls in the school as boys, you will undoubtedly be able to tell me how many boys there are there."

"Undoubtedly," I replied drily.

Can you solve the issue?

SOLUTION ON PAGE  109

THE SECOND CURIOSITY

I was reading some patient notes one evening. I was quite absorbed, so when Holmes said, "I believe there to be a place that is located between England and France, yet is further from England than France actually is."

"Great heavens!" I exclaimed, startled out of my contemplation.

"Not quite," Holmes remarked wryly. "Care to make a more terrestrial guess?"

SOLUTION ON PAGE  110

TRAINS

"**Y**ou know how important it can be to have a clear impression of the way that trains perform in this day and age, Watson. Entire cases can hang on it."

I agreed whole-heartedly.

"A sense of timing in these matters is highly desirable. So pray, consider this little matter. Two trains start on a journey at the same moment, each headed to the origin point of the other, via parallel tracks. When they pass each other, the slower still has four hours to travel to its destination, whilst the faster has just one hour still to go. How many times faster is the one going than the other?"

SOLUTION ON PAGE 110

OVAL

"If I gave you a pair of compasses," Holmes said to me, "You would of course know how to construct a circle."

"Of course," I said, feelingly slightly put out that such a basic matter would even be mentioned.

"I mean no slight, my dear Watson. However, I do wonder if you would know how to construct an oval with just one sweep of the pencil?"

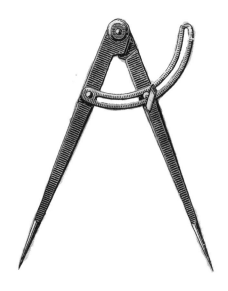

SOLUTION ON PAGE 111

GLOUCESTER

We were investigating a matter concerning a Gloucester cattle-man, a nasty storm, and some peculiar stone shards. One of the elements of the case involved the degree to which the fellow was watering his 'honest' milk.

A maid, tired of her employer, was able to inform us of the procedure. He started with two kegs, one – the smaller – of milk, and the other of water.

He then manipulated the milk as follows. First, he poured enough water into the smaller keg to double the contents. Then he poured back enough of the mix into the larger keg to in turn double its contents. Finally, he poured liquid from the larger keg into the smaller until both held the same volume.

Then he sent the larger keg to London, as the finished product. Can you say what amount of the final blend was actually milk?

SOLUTION ON PAGE 111

WIGGINS

On one memorable morning, young Wiggins, the lead scamp of Holmes' Baker Street Irregulars, put a poser to me after completing some small errand for his master. It is my suspicion that secretly he wanted to put the question to Holmes himself, but either lacked the nerve, or feared that it would be too trivial a matter for the great man.

If the latter, then he made his choice wisely.

"Here guv'nor," Wiggins said to me, "I've got a little riddle. What do you say we wager a farthing on your being able to solve it."

"Is that so? A farthing. Very well. What will you give me if I have the answer?"

"A smile," said the little rascal. "Surely you wouldn't take money from one such as myself, Doctor."

"Very well," I said. "I enjoy a challenge."

"You won't regret it, sir. So, tell me, what occurs once in June, once in July, and twice in August?"

My first thought was the full moon, but I quickly discarded that as not being the case in this year. "Hmm," I said. I could see Holmes' eyes glittering with amusement, but he said nothing, and left the matter to me to resolve.

SOLUTION ON PAGE 112

To Catch a Th

One night in Deptford, we were waiting in a house for a burglar to attend. The man appeared as expected, but managed to turn heel and flee. Holmes shot after him as swiftly as possible.

He returned after a short space, with the burglar in tow. I enquired as to how difficult it had proven to catch the fellow.

"It was a simple matter," Holmes replied. "By the time I left the house, he had a 27-step lead, and he was taking eight steps to my five. It would have been bleak, save for the fact that he is a short man, and two of my strides were worth five of his. In fact, from that, you should be able to tell me how many strides I required to apprehend the scoundrel."

SOLUTION ON PAGE 112

THE SECOND LITERAL ODDITY

I was reading quietly one evening in Baker Street when Holmes put down his violin and turned to me.

"I have another little lexical trial for you, if you are of a mind to accept," said he.

"Of course," I replied.

"Capital. Ponder then upon the words 'cabbaged' and 'fabaceae', the latter being of leguminous fame. What oddness do they share, and why might I remark upon it?"

SOLUTION ON PAGE 113

CHEAPSIDE

We were engaged on some business on Cheapside one afternoon when Holmes turned to me.

"Answer me something, Watson," he said.

"Of course," I replied.

"If there is a fellow whose mother is my mother's mother-in-law, then who is he to me?"

It occurred to me that Holmes must have been talking to Mrs. Hudson again. I put this to him, and he did not deny it, but required an answer none the less. Can you reckon it out?

SOLUTION ON PAGE 114

THE THIRD CURIOSITY

"**Q**uick, Watson!" Holmes passed me a small pad and a pencil. "Write down the numeric figures for twelve thousand, twelve hundred and twelve pounds!"

I paused, momentarily confounded. "What?"

SOLUTION ON PAGE 114

WALKER

Shortly before the tragic murder of the Clapham trapeze artist, I had been watching another aerial acrobat performing a daring routine on a high wire. Armed with only a long, saggy bar, he practically danced back and forth across the hall from his lofty position.

"Daring fellow," I remarked to Holmes as he finished his routine.

"Less so than you might think," replied Holmes cryptically.

Any idea what he meant?

SOLUTION ON PAGE 115

SWINGING PENDULUMS

"**I** have a little physical science question in mind for you, Watson."

I nodded. "I'll do my best," I said.

"Imagine a vacuum jar with a pair of pendulums suspended inside. They are identical, the same size bob, of the same material, at the end of the same length of string. Set them swinging together – with a careful shake, perhaps – and they will move identically, as you would expect."

"Indeed," I said, "I'm glad to hear it, for I would have been stymied were it not the case."

"Now, if you let out the string slightly on one of them, it will slow that bob down, so that the elongated one falls behind the swing of the other."

"Very well," I said.

"What do you think would happen if instead of lengthening the string, I changed one of the bobs for a substantially lighter material?"

SOLUTION ON PAGE (116)

RICE

Holmes and I had sat down to a light supper of bread and soup. I asked him to pass the salt cellar, which was a little out of the way, and he picked it up to hand to me. Then he paused, thoughtfully.

"You know, my dear Watson, we should add a little rice to this cellar."

"Rice? Whatever for?"

He looked at me. "Can you not work it out?"

SOLUTION ON PAGE 117

THE BOARD

Holmes informed me that the senior management of one of the larger London banks had suffered something of a split over a matter of a slightly risky investment policy. Despite a group meeting to attempt some sort of arbitration over the debate, the situation became heated, and a substantial chunk of the attendees marched out in high dudgeon.

"If the chairman had gone with the rebels," Holmes noted, "A full two thirds of the meeting would have left. But on the other hand, had he been able to persuade his putative allies, his deputy and the financial officer, to remain, the departees would have made up just one half of the group."

"I see," I said.

"Quite so," he replied. "Can you then tell me how many men were at the meeting?"

SOLUTION ON PAGE 117

AN ISSUE OF AGE

Holmes and I were taking luncheon when he offered me a test of my ingenuity to season the meal. I accepted, and he posited the following rather remarkable case.

"Let us say that there is a married couple. The wife is younger than the husband, and it so happens that her age is equal to the digits of his age reversed. Given that the difference in their ages is equal to exactly an eleventh of their sum, can you tell me how old the lady is?"

SOLUTION ON PAGE **118**

ALMONDS

fter one particularly successful mission on the part of the Baker Street Irregulars, in addition to paying the three boys involved the agreed-upon bonus, he also gave them a very large bag of sugared almonds, boasting 840 sweets in total.

The boys decided to share the sweets exactly on the basis of their ages, which totalled 28. For every seven sweets that the eldest took, the one in the middle took six; for every four that the one in the middle claimed, the youngest got three.

Can you tell how old the boys were?

SOLUTION ON PAGE 119

STRAIGHTFORWARD

PUZZLES

"The theories which I have expressed here, and which appear to you to be so chimerical, are really extremely practical – so practical that I depend upon them for my bread and cheese."

Sherlock Holmes

THE SIGNPOST

I was cleaning my pipe when my dear friend intruded upon my reverie with what he described as a little test of my ingenuity.

"Imagine that we are out in the wilds of the countryside following a clue towards the solution of some horrid crime, Watson. It should be easy enough to do. Somewhere reasonably unfamiliar to you. Derbyshire, say."

"Very well," I said. "Derbyshire."

"We departed the hamlet of Mercaston at the same time, and made our separate ways into Ravensdale Park. We are to meet in the village of Mugginton, once I've had a look at the 'Halter Devil' chapel. You know that the local paths will guide you between the two, but otherwise you are utterly unclear as to where Mugginton actually lies."

"That takes little imagination," I muttered.

"You are walking along the path when you come to a five-fold junction. There is a signpost which shows which village lies along which path, but to your dismay it has been blown over, and you have no idea which of your four options might carry you to Mugginton. Could you find your way?"

SOLUTION ON PAGE 122

WATER INTO WINE

"Here is a little question for you, Watson." I indicated my readiness to engage my brain.

"I take two wine glasses, one twice the size of the other. I fill the smaller half-way, and the larger just to one third. Then I fill the remaining space in both glasses with water."

"I'm glad this is a theoretical issue," I noted.

"If I then pour both glasses into a previously empty pitcher," Holmes continued, "can you tell me what proportion of the resulting liquid is wine?"

SOLUTION ON PAGE  122

ALBY

"It's like this, Mr. Holmes," said the redoubtable Mrs. Hudson one morning.

"My cousin Alby works at the Millwall Iron Works. He's a supervisor, as it happens. Every morning at 8 o'clock sharp, he makes his way down the stairs. When he gets to his destination a little afterwards, he brews himself a cup of tea, and then settles down with the morning papers. There's a boy who sells them just on the corner by the main gate of the works. I know for a fact that he hardly manages to get half-way through the paper before he's sound asleep, and he remains flat out for the next eight hours. Judgement Day itself would have a hard timing waking our Alby. Yet even so, management are very happy with his performance and the amount of work he puts in. How do you think that can be?"

SOLUTION ON PAGE 123

THE THIRD LITERAL ODDITY

"Consider the humble goatgrass, Watson." Holmes was pacing back and forth in a thoughtful manner, and these were his first words for some time. I looked at him curiously.

"Aegilops is the genus. Bears a striking similarity to winter wheat. Or if Aegilops isn't to your fancy, then how about 'billowy', or 'ghosty'? For that matter, let us not forget 'spoonfeed'."

The penny dropped. "One of your word-plays."

"English is a marvellously eccentric language," Holmes said, by way of agreement.

What is curious about the words he mentioned?

SOLUTION ON PAGE 124

THE TIME

Holmes and myself were making our way back to Baker Street after a disappointingly fruitless day when a fellow across the street hailed us somewhat abruptly.

"You! I say, you, in the odd hat! Tell me the time!"

Holmes looked over at him. "If you add a quarter of the time from midday up to now to half the time remaining from now to midday on the morrow, you will have the precisely correct time."

"I say," the man said, more quietly, and walked on.

Do you know what time it was?

SOLUTION ON PAGE 125

THE FOURTH CURIOSITY

I was engaged in the perusal of an entertaining volume when Holmes startled me somewhat by suddenly pushing my book down.

"Tell me, my dear Watson. By what part does four fourths exceed three fourths?"

"A fourth," I replied irritably.

Holmes looked at me quizzically. "Really?"

SOLUTION ON PAGE  125

A Very Hudson Christmas

Mrs Hudson brought another matter of her confusing relations to Holmes and myself one December evening, more out of a desire to provide us with a little vexatious entertainment I think than out of any genuine uncertainty on her part.

"Gentlemen," she said, "I am hosting a gathering of some of my family this year.
In addition to myself, I shall be entertaining two grandparents, four parents,
one father-in-law, one mother-in-law, one brother, two sisters, four children, two sons,
two daughters, three grandchildren, and not least, one daughter-in-law. Fortunately,
there are no brothers-in-law to deal with. I'm curious as to how many places I need set."

"You'll need a mighty table, Mrs Hudson," said I.

"Not necessarily," Holmes declared.

What is the least number of people that may be involved?

SOLUTION ON PAGE 126

DRIFTS

One snowy morning in January, Holmes paused in the street to bring a curious fact to my attention. Strong winds had driven the snow into drifts along the side of the pavement, but as he pointed out, there was a proportionately far greater deposit of snow against the side of the nearby telegraph pole than there was against the side of the house which lay some dozen or so yards beyond it.

It would have seemed to me that the opposite really ought to have been the case, but after a little thought I was able to demonstrate to Holmes that I could fathom the answer to his satisfaction. What was it?

SOLUTION ON PAGE 126

DAVY

H olmes put his paper down and looked over at me one morning. "You've seen a Davy Lamp, I assume?"

"Those things miners use to prevent explosions, I believe. Basically an oil lamp surrounded by a fine wire mesh."

"That's the one," Holmes said. "They're popular because they won't cause an explosion when brought into contact with firedamp. The ill-educated sometimes believe that the reason for this is that the mesh is too fine for the gas to get through, which is of course nonsense. But can you divine the actual reason?"

SOLUTION ON PAGE 127

THE FOURTH
MENTAL TRIAL

"I was talking to my hypothetical acquaintance Alfie earlier," Holmes said.

I declared that this statement appeared to herald another mental test.

"Indeed. I enquired as to Alfie's age. He, in turn, informed me that in six years time, he would be one and a quarter times the age that he was four years ago."

"I suppose you want me to tell you his age."

"Please do," said Holmes.

SOLUTION ON PAGE

SUFFOLK

"**I** want you to give some thought to three villages in Suffolk, Watson."

I was getting used to Holmes' trials by this point. "Real ones?"

"Real enough, although I am taking flagrant liberties with their actual geography. Consider Crowfield, Hemingstone and Gosbeck."

"They have suitably resonant names."

"Quite. So. Let us say that Hemingstone is directly south of Crowfield, and is connected by a straight road. Gosbeck is off to the east, some 12 miles as the raven flies from the Hemingstone-Crowfield road, and closer to Hemingstone than it is to Crowfield. It is your intention to travel from Hemingstone to Crowfield, but by a slight mishap, you discover that you have instead taken the route via Gosbeck. The roads are equally straight. On arriving at your destination, you discover that the route you used is 35 miles long. How many extra miles did your route take you?"

SOLUTION ON PAGE

THE FIRE

"Ah, here's a diverting little question for you, Watson."

"You are trapped in a small, unkempt valley. It is just a few hundred yards in length, less than that in width, and surrounded almost entirely by stern cliffs that defeat your ability to climb. Some blackguard, who means you ill, has lit a fire at the far end, and the prevailing wind is blowing it straight up the valley towards you. Shelter is not an option. There is no source of water. You have only your usual accoutrements – pocket watch, pistol, notepad, pencil, pipe, tobacco and matches. Can you formulate a plan that will prevent you from being roasted alive?"

SOLUTION ON PAGE **129**

68

THE WILL

Holmes' assistance was sought in arbitrating a rather difficult bequest. He did so in customary fashion, with just an idle word or two, but it was to the petitioner's satisfaction.

The will was made by a man whose wife was pregnant. He knew he would not live to see the child's arrival, and so dictated that that if the child was a boy, he should get two thirds of the estate, and the wife one third. If, on the other hand, the child was a girl, the wife was to get two thirds, and the daughter one third. How one ranks these matters so clinically is beyond me, but that is not the issue here.

However, after he had died, his wife gave birth to twins, one male and one female. The question put to Holmes was regarding how to settle the estate in accordance with the wishes of the deceased.

Can you see a way?

SOLUTION ON PAGE  129

MODESTY

"I was faced with a modest young lady the other day," Holmes said to me. "She was chary of confessing her true age."

"As many women are," I noted.

"Quite so. I was reasonably persuasive on the matter however, and finally got her to admit that she was the eldest of fifteen children, each born with a year and a half between them. When she confessed that her age was eight times that of the youngest of her siblings, I knew at once how old she was."

How old was she?

SOLUTION ON PAGE 130

THE HOUSE

On one occasion which you may recall if you have seen some of my other notes, Sherlock Holmes and I encountered a young woman with a most peculiar problem. She had been picked over scores of other candidates for a position as a nanny just outside Winchester. The one immutable requirement was that she cut her hair to a particular style. She was paid at an exorbitantly generous rate, and given the most eccentric duties.

Her housework was far lighter than any girl would have suspected. Indeed, she was completely barred from one of the areas of the house. So her domestic work was light at best. On top of that, the child of the family was of an age where he barely seemed to need much supervision. In fact, he clearly resented the intrusion. There were times however when she was required to don particular outfits of clothes, sit in precise locations within the house, and engage in various social pursuits. At these times, the father and mother of the house were sociable and jolly. Outside of these times, they were far less engaged.

As if that was not enough to deal with, the house also had a persistent observer, a small fellow who seemed to hang about watching intently at all sorts of queer hours. Strange noises were heard inside the building from time to time as well. The young woman grew increasingly disturbed with the oddness of her situation, and turned to Holmes for an explanation. He was able to provide one almost immediately.

Can you?

SOLUTION ON PAGE **130**

THE BEACHCOMBER

"Look here, Watson." Holmes was standing by the window of our flat in Baker Street. I went over to him, and looked where he was pointing. "This is a rare chance to see a distinctive fellow indeed – an estuary beachcomber."

I looked carefully, and saw that Holmes was indicating a raggedly dressed fellow with rather wild looking hair.

"Look at the deep tan of his face," Holmes urged. "Have you ever seen such a burnt hue?" I had not, and said as much. "No other vocation burns the skin quite so. Have you any idea why that might be?"

SOLUTION ON PAGE  131

THE SEVENTH SWORD

A priceless sword with associations to Mary, Queen of Scots had been stolen from an estate, and Holmes had agreed to lend his services in the matter. The local constabulary was making much of the thief's escape, and sought to ascertain which of the nearby villages was the closest – Shenstone, Rushock or Chaddesley.

The sword's custodian expressed his opinion that it seemed as if all three were as far away as each other, although he had never actually attempted to measure the distances involved. The sergeant maintained that the exact distance was important to know.

It was known that the distance from Shenstone to Chaddesley was one and a half miles, from Shenstone to Rushock was one and three tenths miles, and from Rushock to Chaddesley was one and two fifths miles.

Can you discern the distance from the estate to the villages?

SOLUTION ON PAGE 132

THE WOOD MERCHANT

L ate last August, a curious little incident occurred in Torquay, and an innocent man very nearly found himself the unfortunate victim of a miscarriage of justice. Over the course of one weekend, three local businesses were burgled of a substantial sum of valuables. A number of witnesses reported catching glimpses of a suspicious figure – a distinctive looking man, tall, muscular and well tanned, with a prominent nose and a great big bushy beard.

Local police suspected that the beard was a disguise, and after some diligent searching, they located a straight razor and a mound of facial hair in a quiet nook not far from the rear of one of the burglary sites. Suspicion fell on a local wood merchant, who was undeniably tall, tanned, muscular, clean-shaven and nasally endowed; furthermore, the fellow made deliveries of firewood to all three of the businesses. He had been out of the town over that weekend, and therefore had no plausible alibi.

It was the man himself who made contact with Holmes, laying out the above details and begging for aid in clearing his name. Holmes didn't feel any need to take the case on, but he did send the chap a brief note pointing out one salient fact. This alone was sufficient for the fellow to persuade the police to discount him entirely, as his effusive letter of thanks later attested.

Can you think what Holmes told the chap?

SOLUTION ON PAGE 133

THE DARK MARRIAGE

H olmes waved his newspaper at me one morning. "There is a curious tangle in the announcements today, my friend."

"Is that so?" I asked.

"We have here the announcement of a recently deceased fellow who, so it says, married the sister of his widow."

"What the devil? He married his widow's sister?"

"Quite so," Holmes replied. "It appears to be perfectly accurate."

How is it possible, given that it is not possible for the dead to marry?

SOLUTION ON PAGE 133

THE FOURTH
LITERAL ODDITY

"Time to exercise your writerly mind again, my friend. Turn your thoughts to the words 'scraunched' and 'strengthed'. The former means 'to have made a crunching noise', as if one had walked on gravel; the latter is long out of use, but means, as might be surmised, 'to summon ones strength'. Whilst you are contemplating these singular words, you may also like to think on their counterpart 'Io'. She was a legendary priestess, one of Zeus' many ill-fated conquests in the Greek mythologies."

I confess that I did not reply to Holmes, having been already distracted by the challenge. What do you make of it?

SOLUTION ON PAGE 134

PORT AND BRANDY

"Answer me this," Holmes said to me one evening, as we were relaxing after dinner. "The decanter of port and the decanter of brandy over there are both around half full. Let us assume, for the sake of convenience, that they contain identical measures of liquid. Now, imagine I were to pour off a shot of port, and exactly decant it into the brandy jar. I then follow this action by shaking the brandy to mix the blend, and pour off a second shot, of the mix this time. I finish up by tipping the mixed shot back into the port."

"Sounds like a devilish mess," I said.

"Actually, an even blend of the two is quite remarkably potable. But that is by the by. Do you suppose there is now more port in the brandy, or more brandy in the port?"

SOLUTION ON PAGE 134

THE FIFTH
MENTAL TRIAL

"I was with Wiggins earlier," Holmes told me. "He and a couple of the other irregulars had it in mind to buy a rather attractive ball to play knock-about with. The trouble was that the thing cost 18 pence, and they had only 15 pence between them, all in farthings. They asked for a little assistance. I informed them that if they had sixty farthings between themselves, I had exactly three coins less in my pocket than the average number of coins possessed by the four of us. If they could tell me how many coins I had, I'd pass them a thruppenny bit."

"Did they manage it?"

"Oh yes, Wiggins is a sharp little scamp. Could you have done the same?"

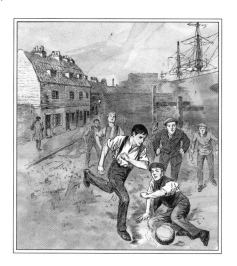

SOLUTION ON PAGE 135

SQUARES

"I have another mathematical conundrum for you," Holmes told me, provoking an entirely involuntary little shudder.

I managed to keep my face from displaying any distress, however.

Holmes, being Holmes of course, had noticed my discomfort anyway. "Fear not," he said. "I'm confident that it is well within your powers. I'd like you to arrange the nine digits in such a way as to have them form four separate numbers, each one perfectly square. Each number from 1 to 9 should be used exactly once, nothing more."

SOLUTION ON PAGE 136

STAMINA

During my military training in India, we were frequently sent on punishing missions to build up our stamina for when we saw actual service in Afghanistan. Those were challenging times, but the sense of accomplishment from getting through the various trials really drove one to excel. As you might imagine, our instructors encouraged us to our best efforts through a system of minor rewards and other inducements.

One particular afternoon still stands out in my memory. We had been sent on a twenty-mile hike through the variable local terrain, leaving shortly before the scorching local noon, with no supplies save a half-pint canteen of water. Our instructions were to make our way round a specific route without stopping for rest or forage; the first man back would win himself lighter duties for the following day. I was stronger then, and put in what I thought was a good showing. By the end of the course, I was as thirsty as a bull, staggering from the heat, caked in dust and grime.

As I arrived, I saw that at least one other chap had narrowly beaten me in. He was in a dreadful state, collapsed on the ground panting, drenched in sweat. Our sergeant was clearly waiting for him to catch his breath. He gave him a few moments, and then proceeded to roundly curse the fellow for a shirker and a cheat, and assigned him to latrine work for the next three days. Then he turned to me, and despite my sudden concerns, told me I was the fourth in, and to go refresh myself.

Holmes understood the sergeant's reaction immediately, of course. Do you?

SOLUTION ON PAGE 136

THE FIFTH CURIOSITY

"I've had word," Holmes told me over breakfast, "of a fellow who has turned up some curious coins in his allotment."

"Fortunate for him."

"I dare say," Holmes replied. "He reports that one of the coins is dated as far back as 51 B.C., while another is clearly marked 'Henry I'. What do you make of it?"

SOLUTION ON PAGE 137

THE SECOND PORTMANTEAU

"**W**atson, are you in the mood for something of a challenge?"

Holmes seemed in high spirits, and was clutching a document of some sort. I allowed that I was game for whatever he happened to have in mind.

"Capital," Holmes said. "You will recall the portmanteau image I brought to your attention some time ago, of course."

"Indeed," I replied. "A composite picture in which each element was a clue to the identity of a certain spot within London."

"Quite. I have another for you, almost as straightforward as the last. In the spirit of fairness however, I must confess that the location is actually slightly outside of London, on this occasion."

So saying, he handed me the sheet of paper he bore. I have duplicated it for your attention. Can you deduce where it points to?

SOLUTION ON PAGE 138

FORTY-EIGHT

"The number 48 is somewhat curious," Holmes said to me.

"Really?" I mulled it over. "It has never seemed particularly special to me."

"Ah," said Holmes, "but if you add 1 to it, you get a square number – 49, clearly – and if you halve it, and then add 1 to the half, you get another square number, 25. There are a multitude of such numbers of course, but 48 is the smallest. Do you think you can find the next larger one?

SOLUTION ON PAGE  138

THE SHOREDITCH BANK JOB

"**I** have a little puzzle that ought to appeal to you, Watson."

I allowed that it was a distinct possibility, and encouraged Sherlock Holmes to go ahead.

"A couple of fellows who are... familiar to me were, last month, discussing the best way to break into a particular bank in Shoreditch. I know for a fact that they even enticed a local constable into entering their discussions, and clearing up some of their uncertainties for them. He was fully aware of what they were about; the bank, of course, had absolutely no idea, and so far as I know, still has no clue regarding their identities. Last week their plans bore fruit, and brought them a substantial sum of money. They duly gave a modest percentage of it to the constable who had been so helpful."

"My word! Have you informed the authorities?"

"I have not, my friend. None of the conspirators has done anything the least bit wrong."

Can you deduce what Holmes was talking about?

SOLUTION ON PAGE 139

THE DAY OF THE BOOK

It was April 23rd, and I was gazing idly out of the window of 221b at the preponderance of St. George's Cross flags which had appeared in celebration of our patron.

"He was from Palestine, you know." Holmes had followed my gaze, and my train of thought.

"Indeed," I said.

"He is much beloved in Catalonia too – where it is traditional to give a book, and a rose. An interesting feature, given that it is also the anniversary of the deaths of both Shakespeare and Cervantes. In fact, they died in the same year too, 1616. It would have been a bleak day for literature... if they had not passed away more than a week apart, that is."

Can you explain this odd statement?

SOLUTION ON PAGE **139**

THE CROSS OF ST. GEORGE

"While we are considering St. George," Holmes said, "I have a little matter for you to wrestle with concerning his flag."

"Oh, really?"

"In shape a centrally placed and evenly sized cross of red against a white field, it is possible – desirable, even – to so balance the size of the cross so that the red fabric occupies exactly the same area of the flag as the white fabric. Let us suggest a flag that is four feet wide and three feet high. How wide should the arm of the cross be?"

SOLUTION ON PAGE 140

THE SOMEWHAT CROOKED BUTLER

"Consider a somewhat crooked butler, Watson.".

I found that image to fit well within my experience, and said so.

"Quite so. This fellow has been drawing off his master's ale. Let us say he fills a generous jug from a ten-gallon keg, and replaces the missing volume with water. Some time later, he repeats the exact procedure. After he has done so, he discovers that the keg now contains a blend of exactly half ale and half water, not unlike that in some pubs of my acquaintance. How large is his jug?"

SOLUTION ON PAGE (140)

CAMPANOLOGY

Church bells are a familiar sound on any London Sunday, often coming from an impressive diversity of directions. I was listening to the soothing peals of one of the churches one morning when Holmes approached me with one of his challenges.

"As a little idle diversion," he said to me, "can you construct a peal for three bells that rings each possible combination once and once alone. Between any two changes, a bell may move just one position in the order, and the cycle must end in such a place that it can repeat without breaking this condition. Furthermore, no bell may be rung either first or last in more that two successive changes."

I must have looked a little daunted, for he added "Fear not, my dear Watson, it is not a trying exercise. Four bells would be a sterner task."

Can you solve the problem?

SOLUTION ON PAGE  141

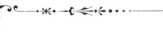

C

One morning, Holmes handed me the following enigmatic message on a piece of paper:

$$1 \quad 2 \quad 3 \quad 4 \quad 5 \quad 6 \quad 7 \quad 8 \quad 9 = 100$$

I looked it over, and asked if it were perhaps some sort of code.

"Not in the least, my dear Watson," came the reply. "It is a mathematical riddle for you. There are several ways to add mathematical operators to this list of numbers to ensure that the statement becomes mathematically accurate. The easiest, for example, is to turn the line into $1+2+3+4+5+6+7+ (8\times9)$. That solution requires nine separate mathematical operators however – one multiplication sign, seven addition signs, and one pair of brackets."

"I see," I managed.

"Permitting yourself just the previously mentioned operators and, additionally, the minus sign and the division sign, what is the least number of operators you can use that still has the sum make sense? You cannot move numbers around at all, but you may combine adjacent numbers into a single value, so that 1 and 2 become 12; this does not cost you an operator."

Can you find the answer?

SOLUTION ON PAGE 141

THE HUDSON CLAN

"Can you sort out a little matter of kinship for me, Mr. Holmes?" Mrs. Hudson had just brought up the morning's post.

Holmes looked up at her with a distracted glance. "I dare say so, Mrs Hudson. What appears to be the problem."

"Well," she said, "I've been trying to figure it out. If Sally Shaw is my third cousin once removed, on my mother's side – which she is – then what relation is her grandmother to my son?"

A knotty problem. Can you find an answer?

SOLUTION ON PAGE 142

COUSIN JENNIFER

One evening recently, after our housekeeper Mrs. Hudson had brought us a pot of tea, she turned to Sherlock Holmes with an uncharacteristically mischievous smile. "I have a little poser that I fancy might amuse you for a moment or two, Mr. Holmes, if you care to hear it."

Sherlock arched an eyebrow. "Go ahead, by all means."

"Well then Mr. Holmes, the long and the short of it is that my cousin Jennifer just got out of London Hospital on Whitechapel Road. She'd been there for a week, and her with nothing wrong with herself whatsoever. No illness, no injury, no mental problems, nothing. Not a word of complaint from her, before, during or after. But they kept her in for a whole week, and wouldn't let her do a single thing for herself. Why, they wouldn't even let her touch a knife or a fork. And to cap it all off, when they finally let her go, she had to be carried bodily from the place. What do you make of that?"

Holmes smiled thinly. "It's clear enough, Mrs. Hudson. What say you, Watson?"

SOLUTION ON PAGE 142

THE FIFTH LITERAL ODDITY

Holmes' next little linguistic challenge came after dinner one restful evening. He had just solved a rather hair-raising case involving a murdered seaman, and we were making the most of a very welcome moment of peace and quiet.

"I have a pair of words for you, old friend," Holmes said.

"Pray, go ahead," I replied.

"They are 'facetiously' and 'abstemiously'. In addition, I'll also offer you the word 'subcontinental'. What do you make of them?"

SOLUTION ON PAGE 143

ELEMENTARY

ANSWERS AND
SOLUTIONS

*"When you have eliminated
the impossible whatever
remains, however improbable,
must be the truth."*

Sherlock Holmes

A MATTER OF IDENTITY

"IT IS VITAL TO SET ASIDE YOUR PRECONCEPTIONS IF YOU are to think freely, Watson. It is the single most important step in accurate deduction. Make no assumptions that the evidence does not clearly support. Louise and Lisa have another sister, Lucy, likewise the product of the same pregnancy. They are not twins because they are in fact two out of three triplets."

A Difficult Age

"OUR CHAP'S BIRTHDAY IS NEW YEAR'S EVE, WATSON, AND our singular day is January 1st. Two days ago, on December 30th, he was 25. The next day, he attained 26. Today is the start of the new year, and at the end of this year he will become 27. At the end of the following year, therefore, he will be 28."

Cold Feet

ONCE I'D HAD A MOMENT TO ACTUALLY CONSIDER THE matter, the answer was obvious, given my medical experience. It is an issue of thermal conductivity. Ceramic tile, like metal, conducts heat very effectively; wool does so very poorly. So when you step on wool, the material is slow to leech the heat away from your foot. By comparison, when you step on tile, it draws the heat away quickly. So your feet stay warm on the carpet, and chill rapidly on ceramic, and you perceive the difference as the materials being different temperatures, even though they are not.

THE FIRST CURIOSITY

IT IS POSSIBLE, BUT IT WOULD NOT BE WISE. THE HOUSE would have to be located precisely upon the North Pole. Such a dwelling would be very cold indeed, and immensely inaccessible.

THE FOOL

IDIOT OR NOT, THE VILLAGER CLEARLY UNDERSTOOD THAT the story of his poor decision-making was the source of a steady, if modest, income. By invariably taking the smaller coin, he ensured that his eccentric legend continued. If he were ever to take the larger coin, it would probably be the last one he claimed, so he continued to accept the smaller, knowing that over time he'd be far the better off for it.

RABBIT RACE

GIVEN THE CONSISTENCY OF THE VARIOUS TIMES INVOLVED, the first three quarters of the race took exactly ¾ of the time – and the whole race took 9 minutes.

THE BARREL

WHAT YOU NEED TO DO IS TO TIP IT ON ITS SIDE JUST FAR enough that the water touches the lip of the barrel," Holmes told me. "Then look inside. If any of the bottom of the barrel is visible, then it is more than half empty. If any of the side wall is obscured, it is more than half full. If the water is exactly at the join, then it is in the precise half-way state."

"And would that be half-empty or half full?" I asked.

Holmes did not deign to reply.

THE FIRST MENTAL TRIAL

HOLMES WAS, OF COURSE, REFERRING TO MY NAME.

WHISTLER

"SOMETHING TO DO WITH THE TEMPERATURE OF the water, clearly," I said.

Holmes nodded. When I failed to continue immediately, he stepped in. "Liquids do not change to gas all at the same moment, nor does water heat evenly. As the water heats up, currents of heat encourage tiny bubbles of water vapour to form. These rise, being lighter than the water, and although some steam starts to issue, most of them encounter colder spots and collapse back into water. These little implosions, taken together, make the noise that you hear as the water heats. As it gets closer to boiling point, more and more of the tiny bubbles survive, and the number of implosions drastically decreases – so you get more steam and less sound. And then the water boils."

"Amazing," I said.

THE FIRST LITERAL ODDITY

AS I'M SURE YOU MUST HAVE NOTICED, EACH WORD HAS THE distinction of alternating consonant with vowel. I have since discovered that the terrible honorificabilitudinitatibus is the longest word in English to do so, with 27 letters to its count, although the others that Holmes mentioned are in joint seventh place at 15 letters in length.

ELEMENTARY GEOMETRY

YOU NEED TO MAKE THE DISTANCE AS EFFECTIVE
as possible, and the means to do so is as follows.

First, plot the relative positions of the warehouse and the dock
entrance, which are not in your power to alter, and then put
in the river. Now, extend a line from the warehouse directly to
the river, so that it hits it precisely on the perpendicular, make
a note of that distance, and continue the line on past the river
exactly the same distance again. You may think of that as a
reflection of the warehouse on the other side of the river.
From that point, extend a second line directly to the
dock entrance. The place at which the second line crosses
the river is the point that gives the shortest route
from warehouse to river to entrance.

The solution works because obviously, any spot on the river is
the same distance from the warehouse as it is from it's reflected
spot on the other side. A straight line from the reflected point
to the dock entrance is the shortest distance – and that marks
the spot on the river bank that is the most efficient. What
is the shortest distance from the reflected warehouse is
also the shortest distance from the real one.

THE MEAL

FOR ALL HIS ENCYCLOPAEDIC KNOWLEDGE, HOLMES possessed some notable blind spots. When I first met him, he even went so far as to claim that he did not care whether the Earth revolved around the Sun or vice versa. Cosmology was always a weakness.

The woman was Eve, and the man Adam. He accepted the forbidden fruit from her, and in eating it, earned the divine judgement of mortality. If he had not eaten, he would have remained eternal. Holmes, naturally, was not in the least bit amused, but I must confess that I did derive some small measure of satisfaction from the incident.

Eureka

THE WATER LEVEL WOULD FALL, RATHER THAN RISE OR
remain the same. Floating, the lump of steel displaces water
equal to its weight; immersed, it displaces water equal
only to its volume, and if it is heavy enough to sink, it is
denser than water, and therefore its volume of water is less
than its weight of water. It simply takes up less space,
allowing the water level to sink.

Regent Street

THE TARDIER MAN PAINTED MORE LAMP-POSTS,
compensating for the earlier fellow's three by completing six.
So the discrepancy is three – but this must be applied to each
side. The tardy fellow did three extra; the early one three too
few. Therefore the tardy man painted six more posts.

RIDER

THE ANSWER IS NOT 10MPH, ALTHOUGH IT IS TEMPTING TO
think it should be.

Let us say the journey is 24 miles. The outward journey, then,
is 2 hours, and the return is three. The average speed then is
found by adding 12+12+8+8+8, and dividing by 5, giving you a
speed of nine and three fifths miles per hour.

Now consider a journey twice as long. Your average speed will be
four hours at 12mph + six hours at 8mph, divided by the ten hours
taken in total – or, again, nine and three fifths miles per hour.

So as you can see, the distance is irrespective. You take
longer at the slower speed, and this skews the average
below the more intuitive even division between the two.

THE SECOND MENTAL TRIAL

HOLMES WAS RIGHT, IT WAS FAIRLY ELEMENTARY.
The midpoint around the clock between 3am and 3pm
is 9am. Three hours after 9am is midday.

THE GANG

"I ASSUME," HOLMES SAID, "THAT YOU TOOK NO ACTION
because no laws had been broken."

"Well..," began Lestrade.

"Tell me, were the firemen rescuing a pet or a child? I suspect
the latter, since they handed the unfortunate to the wife."

Lestrade gave up. "An infant."

THE HAMPSTEAD TWINS

THE CHILDREN WERE BORN ON A CRUISE LINER HEADING from America to Japan. The elder was born shortly before hitting the International Date Line on March 1st; the younger was born a little after crossing it, when the date had gone back to February 28th. Thus officially, the younger twin was born the day before her brother. During leap years, that gap stretches to two days.

THE FIRST PORTMANTEAU

THE LOCATION IN QUESTION IS HER MAJESTY'S ROYAL
Palace and Fortress, famed worldwide as the Tower of London.
The heart of the place is the White Tower, a square moated
keep, although the moat is now dry. The Tower is guarded
by Yeoman Warders, known popularly as Beefeaters, and
contains the Queen's Crown Jewels. Ravens also guard the
tower, and it is said, Heaven help us, that if they ever fled,
the British monarchy would collapse.

THE THIRD MENTAL TRIAL

ALFIE SAT ONLY IN THE SECOND HALF OF THE JOURNEY. In that section, he had to get up when he had half as far to go as he had already travelled – or, in other words, he had sat for two parts of that half of the journey, with one remaining. So he was seated for 2/3 of the second half of the journey – or 1/3 of the whole thing.

CATFORD

THE TEACHER, WHO DOES NOT BOW BACK, SERVES TO counterbalance the fact that each child is not required to bow to his or herself. There are 900 bows, and each child bows once for each other, so there are 30 children, as the square root of 900. As one third are boys, then there are 10 boys, and 20 girls.

The Second Curiosity

THE OBVIOUS TRUTH, OF COURSE, IS THAT THE DISTANCE between England and France varies quite wildly. Between Dover and Calais, it is just 21 miles, but the island of Guernsey, which is undeniably twixt the pair, is 26 miles from the English shore.

Trains

DESPITE WHAT YOU MAY THINK, YOU DO NOT NEED TO know the duration of the journey in advance. For any given ratio of speeds, there is only one spot where the trains coincide, and this will fall in a different relative place. If the trains meet in the middle, they are going the same speed, and have the same time to destination. If one is going ten times as fast as the other, then when they meet, it will be impossible for the faster to have one hour to go and the slower to have just four hours left. In fact, as you can quickly verify for yourself, the one is running just twice the speed of the other, and they have been travelling for two hours already.

OVAL

ONCE HOLMES SHOWED ME THE TRICK, I REALISED THAT
it was a matter of great simplicity. All you need to do is
to place your paper upon a cylindrical surface. The
difference in height will form the oval for you.

GLOUCESTER

WHATEVER THE EXACT AMOUNTS OF THE LIQUIDS,
provided that there is sufficient of each to complete all three
steps, the answer will be the same. The fellow is halving the
amount of milk in the first step, by doubling it with water, and
then doubling the remaining water with the half-strength blend.
The final step does not affect the contents of the larger barrel.
The liquid is just one-quarter milk.

WIGGINS

AFTER A SUITABLE TIME, DURING WHICH I DID NOT
honestly try to beat the lad out of his pittance, I flipped
him his farthing, and informed him he had won.

"The letter 'U'!" he told me proudly.

"I didn't know you knew your letters," I said,
somewhat surprised.

"Ah," said the lad. "You can thank Father Gary on Paddington
Green for that."

I'm still not sure to this day if he meant for the riddle,
or for literacy.

TO CATCH A THIEF

FOR EVERY FIVE STRIDES OF HOLMES', THE THIEF WAS
taking eight, but those eight were equivalent to just three and
a fifth of the taller man's. So Holmes was gaining one and four
fifths of one of his strides for every five he took. The burglar's
27-stride lead is equivalent to ten and four fifths of Holmes'
strides, and it will take exactly six gains of one and four fifths
strides for Holmes to catch his quarry.

So Holmes has to take just 30 paces to catch the villain
– who, in that time, will have run a total of 75 steps.

THE SECOND LITERAL ODDITY

CONSISTING SOLELY AS THEY DO OF THE FIRST SEVEN letters of the alphabet – they are in fact the joint longest words in English to do so – both cabbaged and fabaceae are words that can be played as a sequence of notes upon a musical instrument.

Cheapside

THERE ARE TWO POSSIBLE ANSWERS TO THE QUESTION.
The fellow could have been either Holmes' uncle or his father.

The Third Curiosity

THE ANSWER IS, OF COURSE, £13,212.

WALKER

THE TRICK TO REMAINING UPRIGHT ON A HIGH WIRE IS to keep your centre of gravity directly in line with the rope as low down as possible. The long bar that such performers use provides two handy functions. It is long and heavy, so it possesses considerable inertia. If a performer is wavering to one side, he can push the bar in that direction, and get a stabilising counter-push. More importantly however, the bar has its weight concentrated towards the ends, which dip down and serve to bring the performer's centre of gravity down, ideally below the level of the rope itself. With a centre of gravity below the rope, the performer is far more stable, and much safer, than it may otherwise appear to the untrained eye.

SWINGING
PENDULUMS

"NOTHING," HOLMES SAID. "IT WOULDN'T MAKE THE slightest bit of difference. The mass of the bob has no effect on the swing, as the whole thing is driven by gravity, which treats all objects as completely equal. Resistance from the air might play a part, if the experiment were not being conducted in a vacuum.

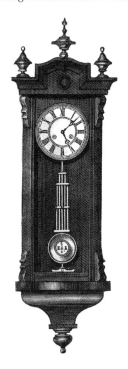

Rice

HOLMES THEN INFORMED ME THAT RICE IS SIGNIFICANTLY
more absorbent than salt, and droplets of moisture will
naturally be drawn to it. As a result, the salt will remain dry.
I confess that whilst I see his point, I'd rather not have to be
picking bits of rice off the salt-spoon every time I use it.

The Board

THE MEETING COMPRISED OF EIGHTEEN INDIVIDUALS.
If three people mark the difference between half and two
thirds, then the total is six times that number.

An Issue of Age

TO KEEP THE DIFFERENCE IN THEIR AGES DOWN TO AS small a fraction as an eleventh of the total, the two digits of each age must be close together. Furthermore, the total age must be divisible by 11. As it transpires, the total has to be 99, and the couple's ages 54 and 45, the latter being the lady's age.

ALMONDS

WITH A LITTLE CALCULATION, YOU CAN SEE THAT IN EACH
cycle, the youngest received nine almonds, the middle one got
twelve, and the oldest had fourteen. The sum of these totals, 35,
goes into 840 some 24 times. 28/35 is four-fifths, which means
that the ages of each child are four fifths of the number
of almonds each gets in a round. So the youngest is 7
and one fifth years old, the middle one is nine and three
fifths years, and the eldest is 11 and a fifth years.

STRAIGHTFORWARD

ANSWERS AND SOLUTIONS

"You know my methods, apply them."

Sherlock Holmes

THE SIGNPOST

"THE MATTER IS EXCEEDING SIMPLE," HOLMES SAID.
"You only have to pick the signpost up and point the
Mercaston sign in the direction which you have just
come from. Then all the other signs will of necessity fall
into their customary positions, and you can easily
discern the correct path to your destination."

WATER INTO WINE

CONSIDER FIRST THE LARGE GLASS. IT CONTRIBUTES A
third of its size of wine, and two thirds of water. The smaller
glass is equal to a half of the large one, so it contributes an
effective quarter-glass of wine, and a quarter-glass of water.
Therefore we have a third plus a quarter of wine, and two thirds
plus a quarter of water. Multiply these values out so that they
are measured in equal twelfths. That is then 4 + 3 twelfths of
wine, compared to 8+3 twelfths of water – or seven eighteenths
of wine, to eleven eighteenths of water. We end up totally
in eighteenths rather than the twelfths we converted
to because there is a glass and a half of liquid.

ALBY

HOLMES CONSIDERED THE MATTER CAREFULLY FOR A
moment. "It is clear that your cousin is an exemplary employee,
so obviously he is not at work during his daytime rest.
I assume therefore that he works the night-shift, and
lives in a converted cellar or some similar basement
abode that he has to walk down to get in to."

Mrs Hudson seemed genuinely delighted to have
her riddle seen through so swiftly.

THE THIRD LITERAL ODDITY

THE WORDS IN QUESTION HAVE ALL THEIR LETTERS arranged in alphabetical order – or, in the case of spoonfeed, reverse alphabetical order. As a point of interest, Aegilops is the longest such English word in the usual direction, and spoonfeed the longest going backwards. If you prefer to exclude words with consecutive repeated letters from the prize, then sponged and wronged must unseat poor spoonfeed.

THE TIME

REGULA FALSI, THE TECHNIQUE OF TRYING VARIOUS
solutions on a speculative basis, works nicely for this puzzle.
Say it's 8pm. Then a quarter of the time from noon is 2hrs, and
a half of the time to the following noon is 8hrs. The total is 2hrs
too much. Try 9pm, giving you 2.25hrs before and 7.5hrs after.
That's 9.75hrs, or 45 minutes too much. So an hour extra is
worth 1.25hrs. You need to decrease the gap by .75 hrs. 0.75/1.25
is 0.6, or 36 minutes. The time is 9.36pm. A quarter of the
time from noon is 2h 24m, and half the time to next noon
is 7h 12m, or 9h 36m when added together.

THE FOURTH
CURIOSITY

OF COURSE, IT DOES NOTHING OF THE SORT.
If you have three fourths, then a fourth is one
third of that amount, not a quarter.

A VERY HUDSON CHRISTMAS

THE SMALLEST PARTY THAT FITS THAT DESCRIPTION IS just seven people – a married couple, the father's parents, and the couple's three children, two girls and a boy. Mrs. Hudson needs to set eight places, including herself.

DRIFTS

THE ANSWER LAY IN THE PASSAGE OF THE WIND. A LARGE, flat surface such as the side of a house is going to divert the wind quite considerably. It has to break quite some distance before the house, in order to flow around it, and this prevents a reasonable percentage of the snow from being flung against it. This is not the case with something as small – and rounded – as a telegraph pole, so the pole gets proportionately more snow driven onto it.

DAVY

"THE FACT OF THE MATTER IS THAT THE FINE MESH
disrupts the flames too much to permit them to escape its
confines. The holes in the mesh are too narrow to allow it to
propagate without losing all cohesion. It is vital to maintain
the mesh in perfect working order however; even one
broken link may be enough to spoil the effect."

The Fourth
Mental Trial

ALFIE IS 40. HIS AGE PLUS SIX YEARS IS EQUAL TO FIVE fourths of his age minus four years. This means that in terms of sheer values, four times his age plus 24 is equal to five times his age minus 16. Add 16 to each side, and four times his age plus 40 is the same as five times his age, or, simply, he is 40 years old.

Suffolk

BY JUDICIOUS USE OF PYTHAGORAS'S THEOREM, AND THE observation that the direct line from Gosbeck to the Crowfield-Hemingstone road cuts the route into a pair of right-angled triangles, the puzzle will quickly fall to our analysis. The direct line from Gosbeck to the road I should have taken is 12 miles, forming the longer line of the triangle with Crowfield, and the shorter line of the triangle with Hemingstone. The sum of the two hypotenuse values is 35, and from this, it is rapidly clear that the distance from Crowfield to Hemingstone is 25 miles.

THE FIRE

AFTER I FINALLY CONCEDED THAT I WOULD PROBABLY BE
burnt, Holmes pointed out that the correct course of action
was to set another fire, a short way down from the unburnt
end. Because the wind is blowing in a fixed direction, the new
conflagration will be driven in the same direction as the current
one. In its wake, the new fire will leave burnt ground. As it
proceeds, I would be able to follow it onto the charred area,
and when the larger flame front arrived, it would be unable
to get purchase in this space. Thus I would create for
myself an island of safety – from the flames, anyway.

THE WILL

TO UNRAVEL THE ISSUE, HOLMES LOOKED AT THE APPARENT
intent of the dead man. This was quite clearly that a son
should get twice the sum of the widow, who in turn should get
twice the inheritance of a daughter. The answer was to
divide the estate by sevenths, and give one portion to
the girl, two to the mother, and four to the son.

MODESTY

WITH 21 YEARS BETWEEN THE ELDEST AND YOUNGEST
sibling, the girl must be 24, and her brother just 3.

THE HOUSE

AS IT TRANSPIRED, THE YOUNG WOMAN HAD BEEN HIRED
chiefly for her similarity of appearance to her employer's
daughter. The unfortunate girl had begun a romance with the
small fellow, a sailor, and the father was violently opposed.
Whilst his daughter remained unmarried, he had the use of her
inheritance from her deceased mother – the lady of the house
was therefore the girl's new stepmother.

The father decided to send the sailor a dismissive message,
and then confine his daughter in a small room at the top of the
house. Holmes' client was there to provide the false appearance
of all being as usual. Apart from our client's original hair style,
the two young women were of a type, and the activities the
couple had her perform were such as to give the daughter's
beau the impression that life without him went on pleasantly.
He didn't believe a word of it, of course.

It all ended well enough, with the lovers free of interference
and married, and our client gratifyingly unmolested.

THE BEACHCOMBER

HOLMES EXPLAINED THAT IT WAS THE SAND OF THE BEACH which caused the intense burnt hue. He was of the opinion that sunlight reflected off the sand far more effectively than off grass, stone, earth or water. So whilst a farmer or a fisherman might develop extensive weathering, only a man who spent a lot of time on a beach would gain that distinctively tanned appearance.

THE SEVENTH SWORD

GIVEN THE DISTANCES BETWEEN THE VILLAGES, THE
application of Pythagoras' theorem will quickly establish the
height of the triangle they form, treating any one of the lines
as the base. If Rushock to Chaddesley is the base, the height of
the triangle to Shenstone is one and one fifth miles. This makes
the area of the triangle twenty-one twenty-fifths of a square
mile. Then multiply the three sides together and divide by four
times the area to get the distance to the central spot, and you'll
discover that the distance is thirteen sixteenths of a mile.

The Wood Merchant

WHEN HOLMES TOLD ME WHAT THE POLICE WERE MISSING,
I found it unbelievable that it had not occurred to me as well.
The wood-merchant was well tanned. It takes months to grow
a big beard, during which time the skin of the face is shielded
from the sun. If he had shaved such a facial adornment
off so recently, his mouth and neck would be several
shades lighter than the rest of his face.

The Dark Marriage

HOLMES EXPLAINED TO ME THAT THE MAN HAD MARRIED
a woman who had died. Afterwards, he married her sister.
When he himself died, the sister was left a widow
– making his original wife his widow's sister.

THE FOURTH LITERAL ODDITY

AS IT TRANSPIRED, HOLMES WAS DRIVING AT THE syllables in the words. Scraunched and strengthed are both single-syllable words. At ten letters, they are the longest such in the English language, although I understand that the American word squirreled is also pronounced by them with a single syllable. It will always be a two-syllable word to my poor English brain. Io, by comparison, is the shortest possible two-syllable word, having as it does just two letters. I must confess to being rather taken with the word scraunched. It has a nice feel.

PORT AND BRANDY

I WAS BUSILY TRYING TO JUGGLE PERCENTAGES AND THE such when Holmes pointed out that the two decanters would both contain exactly as much liquid as when they started. This meant that however much port had gone into the brandy would be exactly offset by the amount of brandy added to the port. I tried his blend, and as he suggested, it was in fact a very engaging drink, albeit a potent one.

THE FIFTH MENTAL TRIAL

I MANAGED TO FORMULATE AN ANSWER. IF HOLMES HAD less than the average number of coins, he had to bring the total average down. The average of sixty farthings across the three boys is twenty farthings each. There could not be a part-coin, so as Holmes' three coin deficit brought the average down exactly, and there were three boys, his contribution was effectively the same as removing one coin from each boy. So the average between the four was one less than it had been, or 19, and Holmes had 16 coins in his pocket.

I forestalled him before he could flip me a thrupenny bit too.

SQUARES

THE SOLUTION TO THIS CHALLENGE COMPRISES
the numbers 9, 81, 324 and 576.

STAMINA

IT WAS THE SWEAT THAT GAVE HIM AWAY. IN SUCH
temperatures, one single half-pint of water is not enough to keep
a man sufficiently hydrated to permit such luxuries as sweating.
Had I been less fatigued on arrival, I would have immediately
recognised that my own perspiration had long since dried up. I'm
not sure whether the chap ahead of me had cut out a large chunk
of the course, or obtained a surfeit of water somewhere along the
route, but either way, he'd broken the terms of the exercise.

THE FIFTH CURIOSITY

IT IS OBVIOUSLY BUNK. THE DESIGNATION 'B.C.' WAS NOT even invented until the year 532 A.D., and when Henry I was the monarch, he was known simply as Henry. He did not gain his appellate 'I' until Henry II took the throne.

THE SECOND PORTMANTEAU

THE IMAGE REFERS TO NONE OTHER THAN WINDSOR Castle, Queen Victoria's preferred home when engaging in Royal entertainments. The Queen herself is shown sitting in a most comfortable chair, indicating that she is both at home and at ease in this location. That alone is enough to narrow the location down considerably. The castle is sited on a small hill above the village of Windsor, and apart from its own architecture, perhaps its best-known feature is the Long Walk, a leafy parade as illustrated, which stretches south for some three miles from the castle gate.

FORTY-EIGHT

THE NEXT NUMBER WITH THE SAME PROPERTY IS 1,680, where 1,681 is the square of 41, and 841 is the square of 29. The next after that is 57,120, and the one after is almost two million.

THE SHOREDITCH BANK JOB

"THEY ARE WRITERS, OLD FRIEND. THIS IS A COPY OF THEIR previous crime caper." Holmes tossed a lurid-looking novel onto the table. "They wanted the details of their story to be plausible. Their book was accepted for publication last week, and the constable who had assisted them with knowledge of proper procedure was fairly paid for his time and expertise."

THE DAY OF THE BOOK

DURING SHAKESPEARE'S LIFESPAN, ENGLAND USED and kept the Julian calendar. Spain, however, changed to the Gregorian in 1582. The date of Shakespeare's death is recognised in accordance with the Julian calendar which he lived under, but if it is adjusted to the Gregorian calendar, it would actually fall on May 3rd. Cervantes died on April 23rd by the Gregorian calendar, 11 days before Shakespeare did.

THE CROSS OF
ST. GEORGE

IF YOU DIVIDE THE FLAG INTO EQUAL QUARTERS, THEN
the difference between the diagonal of this quarter-piece and
half of its perimeter is the required width of the red cross.
Pythagoras will tell us that the diagonal is 2½ feet, and in
addition will confirm that half of the perimeter is 3½ feet.
So the arm of the cross must be 1 foot wide.

THE SOMEWHAT
CROOKED BUTLER

IT IS TEMPTING TO SUGGEST THAT THE JUG WOULD HAVE
to be 2½ gallons in size, but in fact that is not sufficient, as
the second drawing will contain a certain amount of water in
addition to ale. In fact, it has to be two gallons and ninety-three
hundredths to get exactly to a fifty-fifty mix in two drawings.

CAMPANOLOGY

AS THERE ARE JUST SIX POSSIBLE ARRANGEMENTS OF
three items, it is not excessively tough:

1 2 3
2 1 3
2 3 1
3 2 1
3 1 2
1 3 2

Four bells is a little more daunting, but one possible solution is:
1234, 2143, 2413, 4231, 4321, 3412, 3142, 1324, 3124, 1342, 1432,
4123, 4213, 2431, 2341, 3214, 2314, 3241, 3421, 4312, 4132, 1423,
1243, 2134.

C

THERE IS A SOLUTION WHICH REQUIRES JUST THREE
operators. If you do not have it yet, you might like to
take this chance to look away.

No?

Still with me?

Very well. The answer is brilliant in its simplicity.
123 - 45 - 67 + 89 = 100.

THE HUDSON CLAN

SALLY IS MRS. HUDSON'S THIRD COUSIN ONCE REMOVED.
This means that Mrs. Hudson's great-grandmother was the sister
of Sally Shaw's great-great-grandmother. Sally's grandmother –
Mary, as it transpired – would thus have been a second cousin to
Mrs. Hudson's mother Ada, as their grandmothers were sisters.
So moving back down the generations, Mary was second cousin
once removed to Mrs. Hudson, and second cousin twice removed
to her son. Holmes was able to set her straight, but we were
neither of us any clearer on why she needed to know.

COUSIN JENNIFER

IT TOOK ME A MOMENT OR TWO, WHICH TICKLED MRS.
Hudson greatly, but the answer did come to me eventually.
Cousin Jennifer was newly born, so naturally could
not do a thing for herself, nor walk out of the hospital
at the tender age of seven days.

THE FIFTH LITERAL ODDITY

BOTH OF THE PRIMARY WORDS HOLMES MENTIONED contain the six vowel letters once and once only, in ascending alphabetical order, without any repetition. It is my belief that facetiously, at eleven letters, is the shortest such word. Subcontinental, on the other hand, has all five major vowels in reverse order, again once and once alone.

I believe it to be the longest such, provided that one discounts the noble efforts of uncomplimentary because of the out of place 'y' at the end.

If you enjoyed this book,
you're sure to love
*The Medieval
Puzzle Collection,*
also available from
Carlton Books

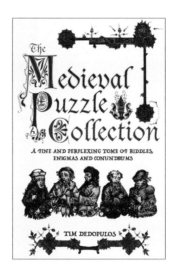

www.carltonbooks.co.uk